The Foster Opossums

The Foster Opossums

By James Byers

Illustrations by Jennifer Houdeshell

Dear Friend,

I'm happy that you have picked up this book because I have a really cool story to tell you.

All I was doing was my daily chore of taking the kitchen trash out to the garbage can. But then my day got very exciting when I looked in the garbage can.

Can I tell you the whole story?

Jamey

One day, a young boy named Jamey was taking out the trash. Hauling a bag of garbage from the house to the large metal barrels on his family's farm was rarely an exciting expedition. But on this day, where his yard met the fencerow dividing lawn and pasture, a thrilling discovery awaited him. Just as Jamey was about to release the trash bag and watch it plummet into the barrel, his eyes caught a glimpse of three teeny tiny creatures lying amid the waste.

Jamey hurried back to the house to tell his mom. When he arrived in the kitchen, he was out of breath because he had made such a rapid dash back to the house.

"Mom! Mom!" Jamey exclaimed, "There are baby animals in the trash!"

Jamey's mother left what she was doing and accompanied him back out to the trash barrels. His mother walked, but he sprinted back to the location of his sighting. When his mother arrived, she peeked inside and said, "Those are baby opossums."

Jamey wondered how they got there, so his mother explained that baby opossums hang onto their mother and travel with her from place to place.

"The mother must have climbed into our trash barrel thinking it would be a good place to stay for a while, kind of like if we were on a vacation and stayed at a motel." She then said, "For some reason, this mother left her children here."

"Why would a mommy leave her babies?" Jamey asked.

"Well, the mother could have gone hunting for some food for her children." his mother reasoned.

And then she said something that made Jamey very sad, "Or maybe the mother was sick or injured and just wasn't able to care for her children any longer."

Jamey and his mother left the baby opossums in the trashcan for a while, but the mother opossum never returned. Jamey began to wonder if their mother had gotten sick. Maybe she really was hurt and couldn't take care of her children any longer. He even thought that the mother opossum knew she wasn't well and could no longer care for them, so she brought them to a place where people could find them. Whatever the case, Jamey knew he needed to do something for the baby opossums, and quickly.

With his mother's help, he fetched the adorable infants from the heap of trash and with parental approval, he placed the three opossums in his hair, yes in his hair! Jamey thought it was hilarious how the babies clung to his hair. Jamey held the opossums and let them cling to his shirt. Jamey's mom took a picture.

At the farm where Jamey's grandmother lived, there was an old barn cat with a litter of kittens. Jamey asked his mother and father if he could take the baby opossums to Grandma's house to see if the old farm cat would take care of these babies along with her kittens. His parents agreed to his plan, but they warned him, "The cat may not like the opossums. We don't know what she might do."

They quietly went into the barn where the cat was taking care of her litter of five kittens. Jamey carefully placed the three baby opossums in the box with the kittens. Then the old barn cat sniffed the new children brought into her home. She proceeded to lick the orphans, welcoming them. Jamey's foster opossums had now become the mother cat's foster children.

Today there are humans, amazing and kind men and women, in the world who choose to become mothers and fathers to children who are not theirs. They care and provide for these children who come from other families. Sometimes it's just for a short time, while their families work through some struggles and difficulties. Sometimes it's just while their biological parents receive help so they know how to be better parents who can protect, provide, and care for their own children. And sometimes, foster parents stay involved for a very long time.

Sometimes a foster home can provide more safety, protection, and care than the child's original home. This does not mean that a biological mom or a biological dad doesn't love their children, it simply means that sometimes they cannot do enough to protect and care for their own children.

Even when we don't know all the answers about why a mom or dad cannot provide the care their children deserve and need, we can always find people in the world who care about children.

Remember the true story about Jamey and the baby opossums? Jamey never knew what happened to that mother opossum. Why couldn't she care for her babies? Why didn't she come back? Some questions never seem to have answers. But to this day, even as an adult, Jamey likes to think that she put her babies in that trash barrel because she knew he would find them. Maybe she trusted Jamey to find her babies a new home. And he did!

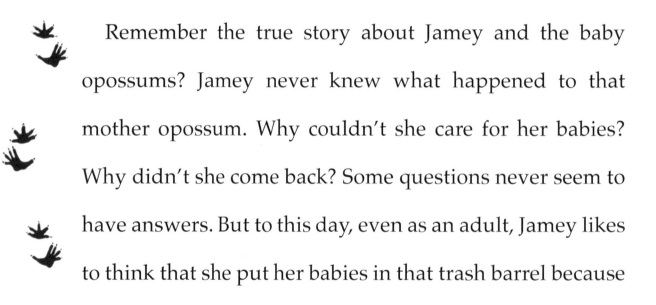

Questions About Jamey's Story and Your Family

There are many different meanings and definitions for the word "family." This is because there are so many different types of families in the world. In Jamey's story, a family was made up of a cat, kittens, and opossums. Maybe you even see Jamey as a part of this special family. How about if we talk about Jamey's story and your family?

- What was your favorite part of Jamey's story?

- What was the biggest surprise in Jamey's story?

- Did any part of the story make you sad? Why was it sad?

- Did any part of the story make you happy? Why was it happy?

The mother cat, the kittens, and the baby opossums made a very neat and interesting family.

- What is your family like?

- How is your family similar to other families?

- How is your family different from other families?

- Are any families exactly the same?

In Jamey's story the mother cat took care of baby opossums from another mother. Who are some adults other than your biological mom and biological dad who have taken care of you?

If you think of your life as a story…

- Sometimes you and your family will have sad pages in your story. What are some sad pages in your story?

- Sometimes you and your family will have exciting pages in your story. What are some exciting pages in your story?

- Sometimes you and your family will have happy pages in your story. What are some happy pages in your story?

Questions About Foster Homes and Foster Families

Foster homes are places with women who offer to be "foster moms" and men who offer to be "foster dads" to children who need a safe home environment. In foster homes the children can be cared for physically, emotionally, and mentally. In Jamey's story, he called the opossums, "foster opossums" because they needed a safe place to stay. The barn cat was a foster mom because she opened her home to the new children from a different mom.

- Sometimes there are different types of children in a foster home: biological, foster and/or adopted children. Were there other young animals in the foster cat's home? What were the other young animals?

- What made the cat's home different from the baby opossums' home, before Jamey found them?

- Do you know any foster families?

- What do you think a foster home looks like?

- How is a foster family *different* than a biological family?

- How is a foster family *the same as* a biological family?

- All children are unique and special, just like the opossums and the kittens were special in Jamey's story. How are you special?

- Foster moms and foster dads open their homes to foster children because they can help care for them and they know they are special. What do you think foster parents might do that makes them special people?

- Do you think you might make a good foster sister or foster brother? What would you do to make someone who is new to your home, feel special?

- Foster children who move to a different home often move to a different school. Would you be a good friend to a foster child who came to your school? What would you do to make someone who is new to your school, feel special?

Questions About Trauma and Traumatic Experiences

Trauma is a word for the severe distress a person experiences following any terrible, frightening, or life-changing event. This can make anyone feel something inside of them. These feelings make us feel uncertain. Our thoughts try to make sense of what is happening to us, and the situations around us.

- Do you think the baby opossums experienced some trauma?

- What do you think that trauma was?

- Have you ever experienced trauma? What was the trauma?

- Did you know that there are people who can help with your trauma?

- Have you ever been afraid of someone, but then found out they were really trying to help you? Who was the person or people who helped you and what did they say or do to help? How did you feel after you received their help?

- In the story, Jamey didn't want to hurt the opossums, he wanted to help them. Do you think Jamey hurt them or helped them? Do you think the opossums feared Jamey? Why or why not?

- Who are all the people and animals who helped the baby opossums when they had trauma?

- How do you think they felt after they received help?

- What clues can you find in the story?

- What do you think you can do to help someone if you know they are going through a traumatic situation?

- Is there something people can do to help prevent a traumatic situation?

About the illustrator, Jennifer Houdeshell

Jennifer Thomas Houdeshell, professional artist and illustrator, does commercial art work for businesses and churches as well as private sector commissions including portraits. Her work has been exhibited in art centers, galleries, museums, and other public venues. This delightful, meaningful story is the 5th picture book she has illustrated. In her artist's statement Houdeshell writes "Art is my affirmation of life and the power of love. It is a spiritual link with my Creator, and a haunting, lilting melody that leads me onward both in times of sunshine and of shadow." Jennifer and her family live in Central Florida where she is actively involved in her church and in social justice ministries. A member of the Society of Children's Book Writers and Illustrators.

Jennifer's website is www.zhibit.org/jenniferhoudeshellartist.

About the author, James Byers

James Byers is a husband, father, pastor, author, and coach. James and his loving wife, Jenna, reside in Worland, WY. Their family combines three biological children and two adopted children, who joined the family when they were 9 and 10 years old. Foster parenting is in their lives by way of Jenna, whose mother and father were foster parents for 18 years. These personal experiences shaped his interest in children and families of foster care. James is an accomplished author, publishing five children's books with *The Foster Opossums* as his most recent and favorite. *The Foster Opossums* is a true story from his childhood experience. His message for communities, churches, foster care workers, foster parents, and families is to embrace and love foster children for the beautiful people they are with the hope of making their current lives better and their futures brighter.

To contact James, email fosteropossums@gmail.com.

The Foster Opossums

ISBN: 979-8-218-22228-4
Library of Congress Number: 2023916378

Perfect Misfits LLC
An Independent Publishing Company
perfectmisfits.de@gmail.com

Perfect Misfits LLC
An Independent Publishing Company

Printed in the USA
CPSIA information can be obtained
at www.ICGtesting.com
LVHW071020151023
761043LV00058B/987